Wait— and See

poem by
Helen Frost

photographs by
Rick Lieder

CANDLEWICK PRESS

If a quick small
movement
takes you by
surprise,

stop and look—
move nothing
but your eyes.

Is that a praying mantis,
brown and green,

standing still,
    trying not to be seen?

It can wait a long time,
staring straight
at you.

Can you wait a long
time too?

If it's hungry
    and it's hunting,
and if you don't
    go away,

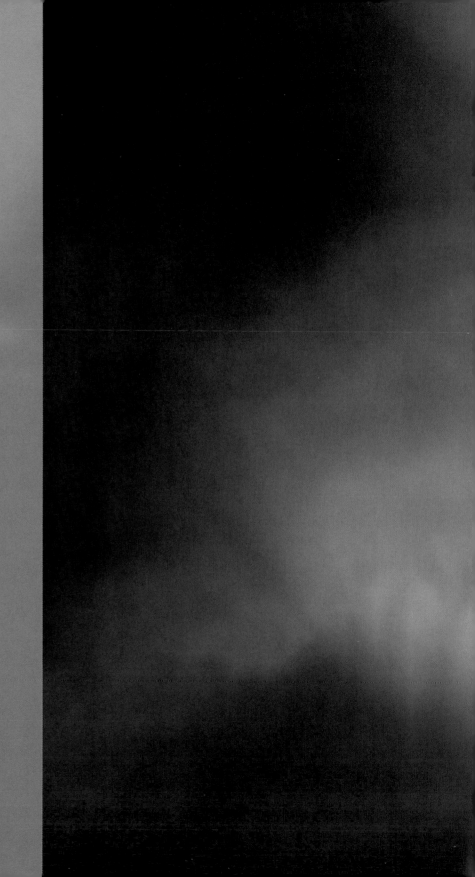

you might see it
make a sudden move

to snatch its prey.

Now that you know where to look, keep watching.

Wait.

And someday,
you may see
a tiny praying mantis
drop into the world.

Then hundreds more.

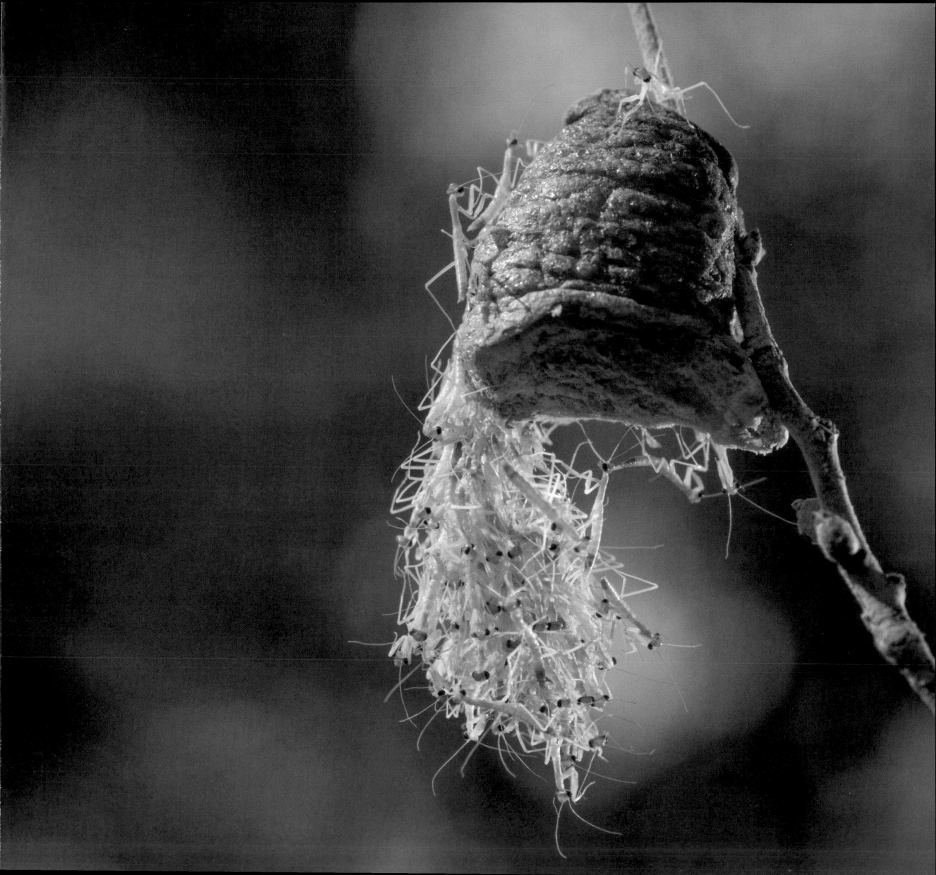

Be still and quiet,

watching,

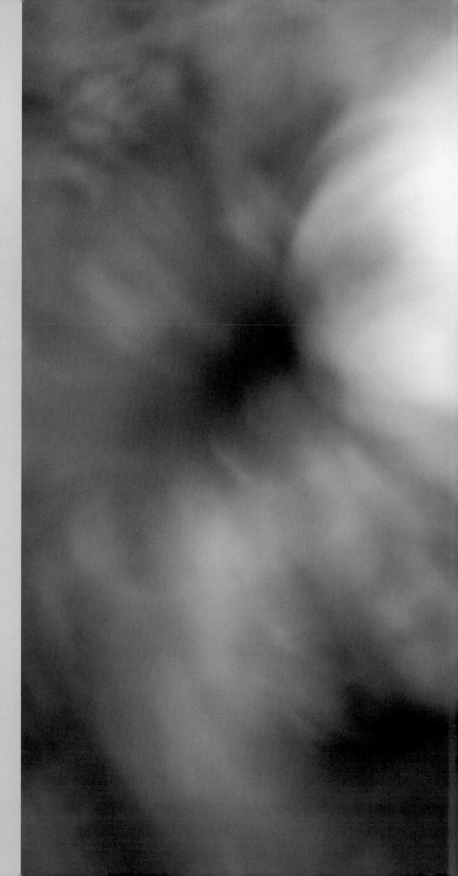

as they step out
to explore.

THE PICTURES IN THIS BOOK SHOW CHINESE PRAYING mantises (*Tenodera sinensis*), one of more than two thousand species of praying mantises in the world. Mantises sometimes fold their front legs and hold them in a way that makes them look like they are praying. But they are really hunting. They turn their heads as they watch and wait for their prey, and when a meal comes close enough, they snap out their front legs to catch it.

Praying mantises begin life as tiny eggs encased in a hard shell, called an ootheca, that is attached to a branch or a stick. If you see such an egg case, light brown and about the size of a walnut, keep an eye on it.

On a warm spring day, tiny nymphs will emerge from the ootheca. Between ten and four hundred of these new praying mantises will drop from the ootheca and begin to walk around as they learn how to find, snatch, and eat other small insects.

The nymphs already have an exoskeleton, a case around their body that quickly hardens. As the mantises hunt and eat, they grow larger, and when they get too big for their exoskeleton, it splits open, revealing the larger praying mantis underneath. This happens several times, until the mantis is a fully formed adult. Chinese praying mantises grow to be about 4 inches (10 centimeters) long.

Adult praying mantises mate in the fall. After that, the female deposits her eggs, along with a froth that will harden into the ootheca, on a branch. She may live for several more months, but she will die before the praying mantis nymphs emerge the following spring.

Have you ever seen a praying mantis? They are hard to see because they blend in with their surroundings. If you don't look closely, you might walk right by one, mistaking it for a stick or a leaf.

Whenever you see something interesting in nature, whether it is a praying mantis, a frog or toad, a butterfly, a bluebird, a skunk, a raccoon, or anything else, keep watching. You might see the same thing again in the same place—or you might not. The important thing is, if you are patient and watch closely, you will always see something that you would have missed if you were in too much of a hurry to notice.

Dedicated with love to Eli Koen, Daniel Benjamin, Titus Paul, Kaden Alexander, and Elliot Ocean.
HF

For everyone who loves a beautiful surprise, and for Kathe.
RL

Special thanks to editor Sarah Ketchersid and designer Hayley Parker.

Candlewick Press, 99 Dover Street, Somerville, Massachusetts 02144. www.candlewick.com.
Printed in Humen, Dongguan, China. 22 23 24 25 26 27 APS 10 9 8 7 6 5 4 3 2 1